THE SECRET TO ENTREPRENEURIAL SUCCESS

How Fulfillment and Focus Can Save a Failing Business

NIKKI G. MEEKS

Published by
M2 Publishing
Palm Bay, Florida
32905

ISBN-978-0-578-40784-5
Cover Design by Ghalib Sajjad
Book Design by Tom Michael
Printed in the United States of America

Dedication

Jude Micah and Chesni-Rae Malonia; you both came along and changed my view on living, loving and giving. I dedicate this book to you both because the change it will create in the life of so many, symbolizes the change you; my children, have created in mine. Mommy loves you.

Foreword

After my first encounter with Nikki, I realized immediately that she is a professional. Believe me, finding professional hairstylists is like searching for a needle in a haystack. Outside of her skills, her professionalism ensured that I discounted the distance I had to drive to get to her salon to get my hair done. I am always surprised at the number of new clients at her salon who says that she was recommended to them by someone. I guess I'm not the only one who hands out her number every time I'm complimented on my locs.

I didn't realize that I needed encouragement to put the final winds in my sail towards entrepreneurship until I read The Secret to Entrepreneurial Success. Implementing just one of the practical "Quick Fix" exercises is already making me excited about the future. To quote Robert Herjavic of the hit TV series Shark Tank "What is great about entrepreneurship is that entrepreneurs create the tangible from the intangible". In this book, Nikki transformed the intangible ways of being an entrepreneur into tangible steps, by using real life relatable experiences and easy steps in accomplishing goals. This book takes away the fluff and distraction often associated with a book of this nature. It condenses strong content into practical steps and guarantees a life changing experience.

While we may not all be called to be entrepreneurs in the primary sense of the word, we should all have an entrepreneurial mindset once we offer some product/service.

Everyone, not just entrepreneurs, will benefit from this book.

-Chioma Aso

Electrical Engineer

Founder STEAMDivas Inc

Table of Contents

Introduction

When I resigned my last corporate job I made a promise to myself to never work for another individual or company unless my own business services were being contracted on a short-term or temporary basis. After 4 years in the public sector as a teacher and 8 years in the financial sector as an insurance professional, I had gotten to the point where I felt like enough was enough.

I had cried my last tear, had my last sleepless night, my last boardroom argument. I was over the feeling of being pushed around and getting the jitters every time one of my superiors rang my personal phone. Stuttering through endless conversations trying to convince *'boss'* on the other end of the line that I was driving profit and that I was gonna get my subordinates to go harder even though I would be chastised if I told them to go home.

I was over the office gossip and the office politics. No longer would I need to prove that I earned my senior position fair and square and it wasn't handed to me because of any improprieties. No more validating my brain-power to those who thought my youth, makeup and stilettos meant I was unintelligent. No more struggling with dinosaurs who could barely construct an Excel spreadsheet but thought their age and tenure made them a better fit for my office. I was done, I was just over it!

I was ready to step into the world of entrepreneurship, I was ready to be a 'CHICK-preneur'! All my previous roles were to build another man's company and regardless of how hard I worked or how much I achieved it was never mine but someone else's. I was now ready to build mine. I was ready to lay the bricks one by one to build my own business and start my own empire. Like anybody who thinks of venturing into the world of entrepreneurship, I was timid and apprehensive but I reminded myself that I already had the know-how from my past experiences and the only thing left for me to do was to execute.

I started a beauty salon with a close friend and I became the face of the salon as my partner settled in another city in the state. While I was given some amount of guidance by my partner, a lot of what I did and did not do were based on my experiences in the education and insurance fields. I found that more and more people I interacted with became interested in what I did to manage a seemingly "successful" business. Many times I wanted to stop them in their tracks and remind them that the business is in it's embryonic stage and it was too quick to attach "success" to the description. I never did, because deep down I knew that the strategies that I was using were going to make the business a success in the not so distant future.

This curiosity from people gave me the desire to share the principles that I used combined with those used by my predecessors and fellow entrepreneurs and create this how-to book to help those individuals who struggle with keeping their businesses open or the individual who is looking to start a business but lacks the know-how and is therefore crippled by fear.

In this book, I outline 12 steps which are necessary for the success of any business; small, medium or large. Each step is explained in a chapter and is backed by my own personal life experiences. Each chapter begins with an opening quote which helps the reader to zero in on the topic covered in that chapter. And at the end of each chapter, there are some practical "QuickFix" exercises which allow the reader to implement what was learned and to do deep reflection on where they are in comparison to where they are headed.

After reading The Secret to Entrepreneurial Success, it is hoped that the reader will have a good grasp on what to do and what not to do when operating a business. The entrepreneur will be guided along the path of entrepreneurship so as to avoid or mitigate the pitfalls which arise when one has made the decision to be their own CEO.

CHAPTER 1 –FUELED BY PURPOSE

"When you stay on purpose and refuse to be discouraged by fear, you align with the infinite self, in which all possibilities exist."-Wayne Dyer

The first step to ensuring success in business is knowing your purpose. Your purpose is your WHY! Why are you in the field that you're in? Why do you get up everyday and go to your place of business? Your why has a direct bearing on your how. Be clear on your purpose not only for being in business but also your purpose in life. Why are you here? So important is your purpose that it forms apart of your mission statement. Your mission statement is a summary of why you are in business, what products/service your business will offer and with whom you will do business. It encompasses everything as it relates to your operations and acts as a means of focusing your day to day business activities around your core reason for existing.

Many people suffer terribly while operating a business and one of the main reason for this is that their purpose was never clearly stated, internalized and understood. If you are not clear on why you are in business, as soon as you encounter difficulties your first inclination is to run. The human brain is as such that when it senses a threat; real or perceived it signals to the rest of the body to either fight or flee. Unfortunately, many of us choose to flee. This happens when our why is not strong enough to keep us fighting. While, if you have a clear understanding of your purpose and you maintain a strong why; you will feel compelled to continue to pursue your goals with much passion and enthusiasm, not fleeing in the face of adversity.

Can you imagine what our world would be like if the Mark Zuckerbergs and Bill Gates of our time gave up on their dreams because they didn't have a clear purpose? When your purpose is established, it gets you through the valleys and atop the mountain once more. What valleys are you going through right now? Whatever it is, I can guarantee you that it is no bigger than your purpose. Having started more than one businesses in the past; I know that the drive needed to start a business is no simple one. Entrepreneurship is not for the faint of heart! Nevertheless, if you have started a business; despite the fact that you may be going through tough times I know and you know that the reason you started your venture is greater than any valley that you may be walking through right now.

As a young life insurance salesman on a day-to-day basis, I had to remind myself of my why, my purpose, my reason for doing what I did. The life insurance sales industry is a very harsh one. One that can turn the sane - insane and cause the faint of heart to have a heart attack. In such an industry, one cannot operate without a clear purpose, a why must be established. It was mid-2011 and I had set several goals that I was going to use to propel my sales activity for that month. It was needed because we were about to wrap up quarter 2 activities and being the super-competitive environment that it was, there were several things at stake.

On this particular day; like always, I got up and put on one of my "knock em dead" suits. If you've ever seen an insurance agent in action, you know that suit! The jacquard long sleeve jacket with the charmeuse inner blouse. This, coupled with my black stilettos and my off-black stockings. I was fresh! I was ready to reel off the 'Importance of Income' sales talk to the first person who said; "what are you selling?" The first prospect that I spoke with had rejected my offer. I went to a second prospect in the same office, she also rejected my offer. I went to a third person in that office - rejected. I remember meandering through the establishment thinking "someone will buy, someone must buy" I had spoken to everyone in that office and nobody bought from me. For a second or two I questioned my decision to walk away from my small but secure teacher's salary two years prior.

I was livid! I was angry and frustrated with the prospect because she told me to come to her office to talk with her yet she didn't buy a product. Feeling dejected, rejected and downright silly I decided to throw in the towel for that day. My first thought was to go home and cancel all other appointments for that day. To add insult to injury, on my way to the car the black stiletto shoes that I felt so posh in - heel fell off. I was walking through the parking lot with my shoes clanking and clicking like a cowboy and suddenly I wasn't feeling as posh as I felt when I started my day. I remember thinking to myself "this is shaping up to be one of my worst days ever." No sale, no heel – no vibe.

I sat in my car for a few minutes and I wondered long and hard about why I had chosen the insurance field. As I reflected, I remembered about the fact that at the tender age of 26 I my earning potential was the same as many Office Managers with years of experience and topnotch qualification. I remembered how my career gave me the opportunity to travel island wide and worldwide. I remembered that through this career I could see upward mobility, put my son through private school and most importantly provide a product that ensured that families were financially secure if the main breadwinner died.

After my reflection, I was reminded of my purpose- my why. I drove out of that parking lot with a renewed sense of who I was and what I was about. I drove straight home but I didn't stay home. I kicked off that pair of broken stilettos, grabbed another pair and headed to the other appointments that I had scheduled for that day. My first response to the situation was to flee but my reflection kept me focused and centered and I decided to fight instead. My fight paid off because sure enough, I made a sale! That month I had one of the best months for that year and was the top performing salesman for that month. So good was the performance I was asked to speak at my company's monthly sales meeting.

Sometimes when we operate without reminding ourselves why we do what we do - we run away too quickly and end up breaking just as we are about to get our breakthrough. Have you ever felt like your business is a failure? If you have; you are not alone. However, it's not hard for you to get out of that type of thinking. You must get back to the basics. Find your purpose because this is the foundation on which you have to build all your endeavors including your business.

QuickFix Activity

- What are your top 3 reasons for being in business?

- If you do not have a Mission Statement for your business, construct one now. Remember, your mission statement indicates what your business is all about to the stakeholders of the business.

CHAPTER 2- FIND YOUR TARGET MARKET

"Everyone is not your customer."- Seth Godin

Who Are you doing business with? It is important that after you have found your purpose you decide who you will be doing business with. You need a target market! Don't be fooled into believing that you can or should cater to everyone or that everyone will want to do business with you. That's not true! Identify the demography that you want to do business with; this is your target market. Business owners make the mistake of trying to do business with everyone and when some people do not gravitate towards their business, they become frustrated. After you've decided what you want to offer and who you want to cater to, research how to cater to that group of consumer. I like to refer to this as my WHAT-WHO-HOW formula.

Your target market must be a group that you are familiar with or are willing to get familiar with. If you are an entrepreneur and you're having struggles with profitability, look back at your market. Sales and marketing 101 - your product is not for everyone! Your product might be outside of the budget for one segment of the market yet not good enough for another segment. Carve out your little section of the market. Decide if you will provide your product/service to individuals or to businesses and then carve out a specific area of the market. This is called creating a niche. A very good example of this is retail grocer Whole Foods. This company went beyond being a grocer and carved out a niche in the retail grocery market by catering to the healthy eater who prefers to buy organic even if it means paying a premium. Like Whole Foods, you can create a niche and then while your business grows you can move from niche to niche.

When developing or overhauling your business plan it's important that you test the segment of the market that you are hoping to cater to. Do researches through your local census bureau and chambers of commerce. I am sure your product or service is needed by a group of persons. The key is establishing who falls within that group and deciding how to attract them to the product/service that you offer. Keep in mind that your target market may be a specific age group, ethnicity, trade group, social class etc.

One of the most significant lessons we learned

as new recruits in the sales industry was that we couldn't speak to 40yr olds the same way we spoke to 20 yr olds. They had different needs. The millennials were interested in wealth building, investing and acquiring assets. On the other hand, genXers were worried about critical illnesses, their aging parents who were close to death and ensuring their own children weren't burdened with their death. We, therefore, had to tailor our language according to our target market.

One of my main target group as an insurance agent was teachers and employees in the education system. That was so because I knew the market. I had spent approximately 4 years in the education system so I spoke their language. I knew the hot topics, their pain points, their likes and dislikes, their hopes and fears. I knew their salary scale and how they were willing to spend their money because I was one of them. It was easy for me to maneuver the market because of familiarity.

However, after a few years in the business, I wanted to grow. I wanted bigger premiums and bigger commissions. I wanted to work less and earn more. So I decided to delve into the small business market. I started to target the owners of small and medium sized enterprises. This dictated that I familiarize myself with the products that would interest this demography. So I learned about estate planning, Individual Retirement Accounts, Keyman Insurance among others. All of these were aspects of the business that I wasn't familiar with but I was willing to learn because I had a goal that I was working towards. This was a challenge that took me out of my comfort zone but it was worth it because my market grew. This leads me to my next point.

Get out of your comfort zone! You can't make money and excuses at the same time. One of my go to quotes for times when my knees start to buckle and I fear stepping out of my comfort zone is "successful people do what unsuccessful people won't do". If the market you're comfortable with isn't keeping the lights on or giving you the income you crave - develop another market. Deliberately search for the demography that will become long-term consumers of your product/service. Your market is what you will use to sustain your business and give it longevity so put the effort into proper development of same . Trust me, I know that there is someone out there who needs your product. Let's find them! And then when you find them, let them refer others. You got this!

QuickFix Activity

- Who is your ideal customer?

- Identify 3 places you can find customers that fit this description.

- Explain 3 ways your product/service can benefit this demography

CHAPTER 3 - BE A SERVANT

"The best way to find yourself is to lose yourself in the service of others." – Mahatma Gandhi

Are you serving the people that you are doing business with? I like to use the term service over customer service. Customer service has become such a cliché term and business owners and their employees believe that customer service is limited to giving hearty salutations, responding to requests promptly and making sure the customer doesn't get upset. Heck! Even some customers believe that's what customer service entails. Customer service is not a department where only those employed to that department cater to customers' needs.

If we remove the word customer and decide to use the term service, it encompasses so much more and it forces us to do more. One of the reasons so many people fail at giving service is because they think that it is a special privilege reserved for customers who have done some transaction with the business. I'm here to emphatically say they are wrong. Anybody who is interacting with your business deserves service. Whether it is the budget conscious individual who is merely shopping around to find the best price or it is the indecisive senior citizen who has returned an item – everyone interacting with your establishment should be served wholeheartedly. After all, the service that you give is what will attract prospective customers or ensure you have returning customers.

Think about the waitress or waiter in your favorite restaurant. He or she will come to you numerous times to make sure that you are okay and enjoying the food. They will ask you to fill your water glass over and over and over. This is because he or she is serving you. This is the true meaning of the word serve or service. I want to challenge you today to fill the glasses of your customers, fill the glasses of your employees, fill the glasses of all the people interacting with your business. And after you've filled their glasses, check if they want more.

In my short time on Earth, I have met many people who have influenced my life and my way of thinking. My friend Borah is one such person. Standing at about 5 feet, 6 inches tall with jet black locs touching her derriere; Borah is a tower of strength. She epitomizes the old adage 'strong black woman'. I like to refer to her as a lioness; in reference to the astrological sign under which her birthday falls; Leo. She is a lioness because she is fearless, she takes charge wherever she goes, she always knows when to strike and she is strong mentally, emotionally and physically.

Borah is the owner/operator of a natural hair salon in South Florida and I have taken so many of my business lessons from watching how she runs her business. She is an astute businesswoman but the quality that stands out the most to me, is her level of service. Despite her strength, she so easily slips into servitude to make her clients happy. Although her opening time is 9am, Borah sometimes takes clients as early as 6 am because they might have a job interview and can't find another time to get their hair done. She sometimes stays late in the evenings to accommodate a customer who gets off work after her closing time. She never hesitates to work on Sundays before or after church or even holidays; just to facilitate customers who have no other available time.

She is loved and not just because she is good at what she does because in that part of town good hairstylists are a dime per dozen. As a matter of fact, she will be the first to tell you that what she does is no better than her counterparts. She is loved because she has a way of never making her customers feel like just a number. This sets her apart in an industry that is saturated with skilled individuals. Her customers all feel like she is catering to them and them only. Because of this, she has a huge clientele that moves with her no matter where she goes. As a result she is able to keep her chairs full and maintain a profitable business.

As I close this chapter, I want to zoom in on an extraordinary act of service and encourage you to strive to be the best servant in your area of expertise. I read an article about a lady who was searching relentlessly for a book at a popular bookstore. The associate searched their inventory online and couldn't find the book, she further searched the storeroom - no luck. Many others including myself, would have probably told the lady that we didn't have the book in stock and moved to the next customer. Instead, the associate did something that was unheard of and way above and beyond her call of duty. She phoned the competition and checked on the availability of the book, it turned out that they did have the book in stock. The attendant went ahead and reserved the book. And as if that wasn't enough, she also printed the directions to the store for this lady. Now if that's not service; what is?

A business cannot be successful without giving service. It is always said that people may not remember what you said or how you said it but they will always remember how you made them feel. When you treat your customers exceptionally, they leave the business feeling good. Pleased people recommend people! Nobody cares how good you are until they know how much you care.

QuickFix Activity

- Identify 2 instances where you think you provided exceptional service to a customer.

- How did that customer respond?

- What are 2 other ways you can offer superior service?

CHAPTER 4 - BE GUIDED BY INTEGRITY

"Look for 3 things in a person- intelligence, energy, and integrity. If they don't have the last one, don't even bother with the first 2." –
Warren Buffet

If you think your business is failing, ask yourself this question; am I operating with integrity? The word integrity is derived from the Latin word integer - which means one or whole. Acting in integrity is, therefore, wholeness and consistency in character. I like to say integrity is what you do when nobody's watching. If you choose to do the right thing when you are alone and not being watched, you are acting in integrity. Business owners today don't realize the importance of operating with integrity. You must be honest in your dealings, trustworthy and upright.

Successful businessmen will tell you that a big part of their success is not them operating with cutthroat practices it was with them doing things the right way. You and I know that there are times when the right thing doesn't feel right and sometimes what we know is the right thing is difficult for us to do. But if you are a business owner who is looking to have a long standing business you have to always choose to do the right thing. The most successful businesses are those that stand behind what they say they will deliver. If a customer expects a certain quality and doesn't feel that quality was delivered then it is your duty as a businessperson to either renegotiate or make another attempt at delivering the expected quality.

Are you an entrepreneur who sets the price according to the type of vehicle your customer drives? Does the quality of your service depend on what side of the bed you woke up on? Or do you make appointments and only the customer shows up for the appointment? Reflect on your mode of operation. Are you businessperson who dodges your taxes and other regulatory obligations? If your character is questionable and double-sided, this may be cause for concern because people will not do business with someone who seemingly has a shady character. Your level of integrity will also determine the level of integrity you get from your staff. Their integrity will match yours because your actions set the tone for the business.

In speaking of integrity, I am reminded of a time when I was trying to find an employee for my business. There is a popular store in the city that I frequented. The employees there are pretty popular around town so I told them that I was looking to recruit a new stylist. One of the guys told me he had someone in mind. However, she was already employed to another salon in the area. He thought that salon wasn't a good fit for her and that she would really thrive more in my environment. So I told him to pass my contact to her and have her give me a call if she's interested. He instead suggested that I call her current place of employment and ask for her personal number.

While I was impressed that he thought my environment was a better fit for her, his suggestion was not doable for me. Just the thought of doing that to another business owner made me shudder. There is no way I could have done that and felt good at the end of the day. I thought about all that time and energy invested in that young lady by her employer and the wealth of knowledge she might have gained from him/her and then to encourage her to just walk away with all of this. I couldn't do that to another businessperson because it was wrong.

Even in times of desperation, we have to operate with integrity. The people who are around you can suggest that you do certain acts to get ahead because they are not fully or even partially invested in the success of your business. At the end of the day, you have to know what's right for your business. Remember integrity means consistency, wholeness, honesty, morality. Therefore this must be reflected in all facets of your life. You are who you are whether you are in the storeroom, the boardroom or the bathroom. Consistency is key!

QuickFix Activity

- Reflect on 2 ways you have acted out of integrity as it relates to your business.

- Identify 1 remedy you may apply to correct these 2 misdeeds.

CHAPTER 5 - OPERATE IN COMPARTMENTS

"It is not that we have too little time to do all the things we need to do, it is that we feel the need to do too many things in the time we have." — Gary Keller

One skill that has always amazed my colleagues, is my ability to deal with only what needs to be dealt with at this moment. It is only natural that there will be various issues to attend to whether in the home, in the workplace or at your child's school. If you are to be a successful entrepreneur, spouse, or parent you will have to learn to deal with these issues on a need to do basis. The art of doing this is called compartmentalization.

In order to maintain your sanity as well as to create a proper work-life balance as an entrepreneur, you must start compartmentalizing now. Imagine a chest of drawers; each drawer represents a segment of your life. You don't go opening all the drawers on a chest all at once. No, you only pull the drawer that you need to open at present. This is similar to your life. While you are at work leave the family issue drawer closed. Do not open it until you are able to handle the issue wholeheartedly and effectively; chances are that would be after you have left work.

The year 2012 was a tremendously trying year for me. I was at the peak of my insurance career after having qualified for and attended the Million Dollar Round Table in Anaheim, California. This was the premier conference for the top sales professionals worldwide. My work life was doing great, however, my home life was in shambles. My marriage of 7 years was about to end. We both tried to save it, especially because we had a 4-year-old child who would be affected by this split.

The truth is, not many people in my work environment really knew about what was happening in my home life. I made every effort to function at the level at which I usually did. I didn't have meltdowns and outbursts-in public!. My poor performing months were never because I was dealing with a separation, it was because I didn't do enough. I had to truly exercise my emotional intelligence during this period.

And as if a separation wasn't a big enough blow, 2 months later my grandmother who I spent half my life with got an aneurysm and died suddenly. It was indeed some trying times. I remember staying up some nights crying not even sure if I was crying for the marriage or my grandmother. I was sad. However, at the crack of dawn every day I was up being a mother to my 4 years old who was miserable that he wasn't seeing daddy anymore. I made the decision to thrive even in my misery.

That year I lost my marriage, my child's father and my grandmother but I broke a company record, was one of the top 2 salespersons for my company and qualified for Million Dollar Round Table again! As an entrepreneur, compartmentalization is key because it doesn't only allow you to focus, it also gives you the strength to deal with life's knockdowns. There is a little quote I would repeat to myself on the days when I felt it was too much and I just wanted to lock myself in my bedroom and cry; "get up, dress up, show up". I learned it from my first branch manager when I entered the insurance industry. It helped me to survive 2012 because every day I would get up as early as I could, dress up in my suits; makeup, best hair, stilettos and show up to my prospects to close yet another sale.

Have you been opening too many drawers at once? If you have, this may be the reason or one of the many reasons you are struggling with finding entrepreneurial success. Be kind to yourself, there is only one you. While society glorifies the ability to multitask especially for females, we must never bite off more than we can chew at any one time.

QuickFix Activity

- Think of 4 stressful situations in your life currently and order them according to priority and decide where and when you will attend to each.

- Write your answers down for accountability.

CHAPTER 6- SET S.M.A.R.T GOALS

"What keeps me going is goals." — Muhammad Ali

Goal setting is very important to every business. So important is goal setting, it is the first thing one should do when starting a business. If you think you can operate a business without goals …. try getting a start-up loan or attracting investors. One of the first things requested is a business plan. Your business plan acts as your blueprint. It outlines all that you expect to get out of your business as well as all that you intend to put into the business. When you are setting your goals it is important that you set smart goals. SMART is an acronym for the structure of your goals.

"S" means your goals must be specific; Many entrepreneurs mistake their dreams for goals. Dreams are hopes and aspirations, however, goals are the steps that you will take to achieve these aspirations. Hence the need for your goals to be specific. Therefore, instead of saying I want to be the best barber in town be specific and say I want to be able to cater to all hair types and as such be widely known for my skills and ability. When specificity is added to a dream, it gives you something to work towards.

"M" means measurable; your goal must be able to be measured for you to be able to decide whether or not the goal has been achieved. It is said that if it cannot be measured, it cannot be managed. Therefore, a metric must be added to your goal eg. I want to add 2 new customers and reconnect with 1 existing customer every weekday.

"A" means attainable; a goal that is attainable is one that you are able to achieve. It cannot be a pie-in-the-sky dream that you and everyone else know will not come to fruition. While your goals should be big enough to stretch you it should not be too far above reality. Instead, it ought to be doable and realistic.

"R" means relevant; it is important that your goal is relevant to your situation. Your goals should help you to move towards the big dream. Therefore, if you dream of being the most popular barber in your area you don't need to have a goal to tailor 8 men's pants every day. While it might be a side hustle, you have to focus on the dream and set your goals accordingly.

"T" means time-bound; you need limits, you need boundaries. Unless you set up a time by which you want to achieve your goals, your mind will tell you that there is always enough time when there isn't. For you to reach the dream, you must do everything in a timely fashion or else 10, 15 or 20 years from now you will still be in a rut trying to figure out the dream you have.

Setting SMART goals help to hold you accountable and gives you a push. If you know you are working with a pre-defined time period you will undoubtedly work with some amount of urgency and it will allow you to better evaluate your progress.

When I attended teachers' college in Jamaica, we were taught the keys to setting goals and it almost always came down to writing SMART goals. As such, when I moved into the field of business, I also carried this strategy with me. It's the secret sauce that always set me apart from my counterparts, helping me to get ahead and realize my dreams.

QuickFix Activity

- Review or create 4 business goals for this year. Use the SMART goal writing strategy.

CHAPTER 7 – CRYSTALLIZE YOUR GOALS

"Crystallize your goals. Make a plan for achieving them and set yourself a deadline." – Paul Meyer

While goal setting can be one of your biggest weapon in the business arena, it can sometimes make you feel like you are getting beat down if you are not meeting your goals. I have found that most persons who find it difficult to achieve their goals do not crystallize their goals. In essence, the term crystallizing your goals means you are going to become definite about your goals and their achievement. Its where you add clarity and certainty to the goals.

When I entered the life insurance industry I remember hearing my branch manager talk a lot about crystallizing our goals. I didn't ever pay too much attention to the term until years after when I had become an aggressive insurance salesman searching for new ways to get to and remain at the top. I found myself breaking my monthly goals further into weekly goals and then into daily goals. I didn't stop there! Now, this is where it got crazy – I would literally break my daily goals into the commission that I wanted to earn from each policy sold. This allowed me to have clarity when I started my day. So I knew exactly which plans I wanted to sell and as such I knew who I needed to target to sell those plans.

Pen and paper were my best buds. I wrote everything down from the big monthly goal to the small daily goal. Studies have shown that people who write their goals down are more likely to achieve their goals because writing helps the brain to filter important things -*like your goals* from unimportant things. Have you ever noticed a quarter back during a football game? They have their plays written on their wristband. Writing does a lot for the human brain. I would write my goals on sticky notes and put them all over my bedroom and bathroom. It was a constant reminder and a means of remaining accountable.

Crystallizing my goals gave me a definite game plan for each day. And having a game plan gave me strength on those days when I felt weak and pushed me to "get up, dress up and show up". I used this method to ensure that even if I didn't achieve said goal, I would realize a large portion of that goal. This strategy kept me ahead of the game most times and always left my counterparts wondering what I was doing differently.

QuickFix Activity

- Break down your goals from chapter 6 into small portions that are achievable on a daily basis.

- Describe the who, what, where and how when creating this plan.

CHAPTER 8- EVALUATE YOUR PROGRESS

"Evaluate what you want-because what gets measured, gets produced."- James A. Belasco

After you have set your goals and ensured that they are SMART goals you must evaluate. One of the biggest problems faced by business owners today is that we do not evaluate, we do not check where we're at compared to where we started. We forget to check if we are on target as it relates to what we set out in the business plan. Sometimes a business owner may have deviated from their blueprint and it's the evaluation process that is going to point this out. It will make you see where you need to start over or edit instead of continuing blindly along the wrong path.

For small business owners, it might be a little tedious to have designated periods for evaluation. However, in order to properly execute your strategies to achieve your goals, a minimum of 4 evaluation periods must be worked into the business year. In order for you to be able to properly evaluate, there are several key actions that must be taken on a daily basis. These are recordkeeping, analysis of data and acceptance of feedback. Evaluation as a process should look at more than the success of the business. It should look at the output from employees as well as the input of the business owner. Writing down information on a daily or at least weekly basis will also assist you in this endeavor.

As a business owner, it wasn't always easy to

have meetings with my staff or even my business partner due to location constraints. So I would just do quick polls with customers or staff while carrying out everyday activities. I weaved it into my conversations so it didn't appear too much like an evaluation was being done. When we opened the salon we did several methods of marketing to ensure our name was in the marketplace. However, we didn't know exactly which worked and which didn't. So in an effort to get insight, each time a new customer sat in my chair I would ask them at some point in our conversation "how did you hear about us?" This worked wonders because it made me realize the level of impact our service had on our customers. Most persons told us that they found us on Google and they chose us based on the number of positive reviews. This is data I was acquiring and I would be able to make decisions based on this feedback. This meant our paid ad on Google was working and this is one method of marketing that should be continued and expanded if possible. Good reviews meant that we were giving good service and the employees needed to be commended.

For smaller businesses, the structured evaluation may not be possible but you can definitely use quick informal polls to see if you are indeed achieving your objectives.

QuickFix Activity

- Identify 3 ways you can evaluate progress or lack of progress in your business.

- What are the metrics used to do this evaluation?

CHAPTER 9 – ATTRACT WHAT YOU WANT

"Everything you want, also wants you" Jack Canfield

Let me be bold and say, whatever is happening in your life right now is as a result of what you're thinking and feeling. If you have a business that is not doing well, *(I know I may become the enemy right now for telling you that it's your fault but I'm going to do it anyway)* it's your fault. This is because like attracts like and you become what you think about. Your supposed failure means your energy is out of alignment with your dreams. Have you ever woken up and had one bad situation and you responded to it by saying "today's going to be a bad day" or "this is going to mess my day up"? And as luck would have it everything goes wrong for that day? That is because you requested a bad day and the universe responded accordingly. You activated the law of attraction – but in a negative way.

The law of attraction states that you ask for what you want as opposed to what you don't want. Human beings possess what is called ENERGY. Your energy attracts like energy and as such whatever frequency you are in, you will attract the experiences and opportunities that are in alignment with that frequency. Another component of attracting the life you want is to live in the now. In other words, act like you already have what it is you want. See, when you do this the brain searches for the opportunities, ideas and situations which will actually make your thoughts a reality. Therefore if you want to be a winner in the business arena you must ask for exactly that and begin to act like a winner, think like a winner, feel like a winner. Your words and thoughts must portray winning, so instead of saying I don't want to fail, change your language to I will be a success. Both statements portray the same idea but both are going to get different results from the universe because the brain will process the operative words; success or fail.

As a business person the law of attraction is an important part in your success or lack thereof. When you create your goals for your business you need to do so with the law of attraction in mind. You must identify that which you want and the brain will react in such a way that it pushes you towards exactly that. It forces you to think outside of the box and come up with ideas and solutions that you would not have thought about under ordinary circumstances.

I recently stumbled upon a photograph that I had as my wallpaper on my phone in 2013 when I was offered a Trainer position with a company I had worked for then. I had been in insurance sales for a few years and I was becoming burnt out. I always wanted to be an industry trainer because teaching and insurance sales were my two loves and really the only careers that I knew. I thought if I merged both then that would be my ideal career, it would essentially make me happy and give me the feeling of self actualization. I applied to a few insurance companies however there was no response – like literally none! Nada! Zilch! So I licked my wound and I moved on, I left the business for some months.

As luck would have it and by some strange twist of fate I was at a friend's party and I saw my former boss. I was happy to see him – not because I was thinking of a rehire or anything but because I had genuinely missed the comradery. He came over to me and I remember his words clearly "can you do some training in Mobay for me?" Mobay is the shortened form of Montego Bay which is Jamaica's second city.

When this happened, I was shocked yet happy all at once– really I don't know why because the universe never fails! While I was expecting the positive, the enchantment of the whole situation just had me in awe. The picture that I had as my phone wallpaper, was of a female standing in front of a room full of adults some with their hands raised while she was writing on a white board. I was getting my dream without sending out a million job applications, flustering through interviews or sitting by the phone for hours expecting a call back. Take a minute and process what you just read - because this might be mind-blowing to you but only because you don't know the power of the human brain.

He had recently opened a branch in that part of the island and needed assistance with training the staff and I was looking to go into the next chapter of my career so I was on the lookout for training opportunities. The frequency on which I was operating aligned with his and although at the beginning of the story I said "as luck would have it", this was no luck- it was the law of attraction and the law of visualization at work. To the average man this might seem purely coincidental but to the individual who understands the laws of the universe - this is the answer to what was requested.

We all possess energy, so do not think that this is some supernatural power that only some people possess. You can begin to attract the things that you want; your dreams, your aspirations. Its out there waiting for you to get into alignment. You are the creator of your life and whatever you request; you not only deserve but you will get. Stop putting out fear and failure into your atmosphere and start putting out faith and focus. Don't think about what may go wrong or have gone wrong. Think about what can go right or has gone right. All the successful businessmen of our time have used the law of attraction and attributes their success mainly to the thoughts and feelings they harbored.

QuickFix Activity

- Identify 3 thoughts you harbor that may be attracting negative results in your business.

- Write these down and put a strike

through the word wont, don't or can't in each statement.

- Rewrite these statements using the word will or can.

- Create a board /wall by cutting pictures of 6 things you see in your life in the next 2 years. Paste these pictures onto your board/wall. This is your vision board. Do some research on how to create the ideal one.

CHAPTER 10 – ASK WITH EXPECTATION

"What you expect to happen, eventually happens" Meghan Olsgard

It is all good and well that you ask the universe for what you want but asking is nothing if you do it without expectation. Expectation is directly tied to requesting or asking for what you want. Society has taught us that expectation leads to disappointment. We therefore leave our aspirations hanging, hoping they will be manifested but never truly feeling and believing that they will. It is important as individuals and as business people that we understand that whatever we request of the universe will be done only if we expect it to be done. The law of attraction is way more than just requesting and thinking positive thoughts. The law of attraction runs parallel to expectation. Therefore, if you ask and you expect a positive outcome in the future it will drive you to take action. The brain will automatically think of ways to get the specific outcome.

Expectation is tantamount to faith but contrary to popular belief faith alone doesn't get you anywhere; works is also needed because faith without works is dead. If you ask without expectation, you will not have the drive to take action because you already do not expect a positive future outcome. Your expectation reflects in the way you make your requests. As an avid believer in the law of attraction I have come to realize that my language plays a big part in my request, expectation and outcome. For example, instead of saying "I hope I earn $300 today" restructure your request to suggest that you are expecting $300 today – say "I am happy I am making $300 today". Automatically you will expect to have a $300 income at the end of the day and as such the brain will push you to work towards that outcome.

Remember the Trainer position I told you I manifested in 2013 – I expected it. Prior to attending the party, I had spent some vacation time with my friend in South Florida. While I was clothes shopping to return to Jamaica, my friend made a mockery of me. She laughed at me so badly- I was unemployed yet I was buying office wear. She found it strange and funny at the same time that I was spending money on office wear and I did not have a job. While it was all in jest and we enjoyed the light laughter, there is a lesson to be learnt. When you begin to live your life with positive expectancy, much of your actions will not be understood by others but do it just the same! Some people may even believe that you should be on psychiatric medicines and that's ok, just keep expecting and remain convicted that you will see a positive outcome. My expectation led to me being prepared when the opportunity came.

I know that for many of you, expecting a positive outcome comes naturally. Scientists call this the 'Winner-Effect'. Studies in animals have shown that when animals (including human beings) win at something, their brains release the hormones; testosterone and dopamine. When this happens repeatedly, the chemical structure of the brain morphs making these animals smarter, more confident and more successful in the long run. On the contrary, animals that fail at a task go on to fail repeatedly and sometimes even more catastrophically and this is because past failure impedes concentration. That's the scientific explanation but it really just comes down to expectation.

If you expect to fail because of past failures – you will fail. If you expect to succeed because of past successes – you will succeed. When these are repeated overtime, it becomes a pattern. This is why Usain Bolt continuously won gold medals and broke records while Asafa Powell continued to get injured on the big stage. So if you are used to messing up and are sitting, waiting to fail- stop now. Turn off the negative radio in your head and turn on the positive one. You will be successful, tell yourself that you will. Consider all your past disappointments as teachers and take the lessons from each because in life there is no losing. You either win or you learn.

QuickFix Activity

- Reflect on 2 things you have requested. Have you been expecting a positive result? If not, raise your level of expectation now.

CHAPTER 11 - BE GRATEFUL

"Gratitude turns what we have into enough" Melody Beattie

Have you ever spoken to someone and when you hear their story you became content with your problems? Suddenly, the mountain of problems you have, appear to be a molehill. It is important that we have what is called gratitude. You may feel as though because you are not earning a six figure income consistently or instantly, your business is failing or you are not doing well. That's not true! Whenever you get into that mode where you feel as though nothing is happening for you remind yourself that somebody out there is in a worse position. Begin to be grateful for what you have and for where you are in the process.

Many times we compare our business with other businesses not realizing that both businesses are at different stages in the developmental process. There is no way a business that is 1 year old can function like a business that is 7 years old. One is in an embryonic stage and the other is budding into maturity. The former is concerned with acquiring a client base and assets while keeping the doors open by taking care of the month to month overheads. The latter, is at a stage where the business may have a steady client base and now needs to focus on cash flow or balancing income and expenditure. Many start-ups fail for this reason. It's therefore necessary for us to determine the stage that our business is at whether it is determined by the period of existence or annual sales and know what to expect at this stage.

Before I entered the life insurance business I was sold the idea that life would turn around. I believed I would be driving a brand new car in a short period of time or buy a new house in a short period of time. I was supposed to be a new person! I was sold a pipedream or maybe I should say I bought a pipedream. These promises seemed very feasible because most of the sales agents at my company seemed to be doing well. And so I was looking at them thinking that things would be the same way for me as soon as I entered the business. When I started the business in 2009 I owned a 14 year old car and of course I thought my car was not flashy enough to go into the field and do business. If you know anything about the sales aspect of finance you will know that you need to look like what you're selling. So if you sold products that would make life better for people there was no way you could be looking like life isn't good for you!

To keep up with my colleagues, I decided it was time to acquire a new vehicle. I began to seek sale for my old car just 4 months after entering the business. I was measuring myself against those sales agents who had been in the business for 5, 10 or 15 years and had gotten to the point where they could drive what could be described as a nice vehicle. I thought that after 4 months I could be on the same level with them; that was a big mistake! Not that this was impossible because I have seen salesmen come into the business and hit it big after 2 or 3 months. It's just that, this was not the trajectory that my career was on. I had to start with baby steps.

I went ahead and applied for a loan but the bank did not approve my loan for obvious reasons. After all, I was only in the job for 4 months, I was commission-paid, I was a contractor and not a permanently employed staff. There was a whole list of valid reasons why this loan was really not the best thing for me or the lender at that point in time. Looking back, I remember getting this sinking feeling in my stomach – you know, the feeling you get after being punched.

Do you remember that I said I sought sale for my 14 years old car? Well I had sold it, just before the bank made a decision on the loan. So with the loan being denied, it meant I had gone from having a functioning vehicle to only having 2 functioning feet and the job needed to be done despite my self-inflicted miserable situation. That was one of my first lessons on gratitude in the early stages of my career. You're wondering how I did it right; I took taxi, walked and hitched a ride here and there until I was able to get a replacement vehicle. So, the funny part of the story is that when I eventually got a replacement vehicle I ended up buying a 17 years old vehicle- out of desperation. What I had taken for my 14 years old vehicle was not enough to get another one of the same age. Talk about jumping out of the frying pan and into the fire!

Remember in life there are no losses; you either win or you learn. I sure learnt from this situation. After a few months passed I was so happy that the loan was not granted because after the first 6-8 months in the business it was not what I expected it to be monetarily. Sure there were good months but there were also some very rough months as is customary with commission sales. Truth is; anyone who has ever done sales knows that it's a process. Well, unfortunately I didn't know because this was my first sales job plus I was young and naïve! It wasn't until my fourth year in the business that I was able to purchase a newer vehicle and it wasn't even brand new. I was able to truly smell that new car smell and remove the plastic from the seats after all of 6 years in the business.

The lesson in the story is; whatever business you are in, never use your counterparts as a measuring stick. Stay in your lane! Each stage of your evolution has different characteristics; enjoy it and trust the process! Now I know this is hard to do especially when you have big dreams and social media is dictating what our lives should look like. However, a spirit of gratitude is what will take you through this phase. While you are waiting for the big break be grateful and acknowledge small wins!

QuickFix Activity

- Identify 4 things that you are grateful for at this stage

CHAPTER 12 - CREATE A MASTERMIND GROUP

"Sticks in a bundle are unbreakable" Kenyan Proverb

The single most common action among successful people is their ability to find people who are a lot like them. Your circle of friends is a crucial part of your success or failure. Along with your optimistic friends, you need to seek out mentors. These are people who you admire and they are where you would like to be. These individuals are going to coach you in the areas that you need the most guidance. In essence, you create a mastermind group. You cannot have big dreams but hang around small minded friends. If you have caviar dreams, you can't hang out with the sardine gang!

When you are going through tough times it's imperative that you have a strong support system. It is often said that no man is an island and it may sound cliché to you but it is a real fact. What may seem insurmountable to you alone will seem like a walkover for a group of 4 friends. This is where your mastermind group becomes important because they are the ones who will help you through your valleys. Jim Rohn pointed out that we are the sum of the 5 people we spend the most time with. Who are you spending your time with? Are they uplifting or demeaning? Are they positive or negative? Are they optimistic or pessimistic? Do they deposit in your life or they do withdrawals? These are all questions you have to ask yourself in order to do a true assessment of your 'POWER POSSE'.

When I reflect on my life, the times when I have truly fallen down and made not so brilliant decisions are those times when my friends and associates were on different wavelengths from me. There are some friends that suck the blood out of you! You know them! Those who tell you every reason your plans will not work and every reason your dreams will not come through. Be wary of them because over time you begin to think like them, walk like them and talk like them. They are going to help you down. I know you might be thinking that you are mentally tough and cannot be affected by their negativity. That's what I thought too! I was wrong and if you are thinking the same thing – you are wrong too.

I had a friend some years ago, we entered our sales career at the same time. After reality hit us and we realized that sales was not a get rich quick scheme, we sought solace in each other's company. We started to call each other every night after work, we were going out together and sometimes even prospecting together. Over time our conversations became centered around one topic and that's how much sales was not working for us. Everyday we would joke about how we had options and unlike the star performers we had other careers that we could pursue; for her it was banking and for me it was teaching. Together, we became cynics, no longer seeing the job as doable or even worth doing. We became Negative Nancy 1 and 2, frequently having our pity parties that lasted for hours at a time. Needless to say, we both did poorly and eventually left the business. I was able to find my way back but she wasn't able to do so.

Months after, when I did my own introspection I realized that my choice of company was one of my primary downfall. I went wrong in 2 ways and I tried to never make an error such as this in future. Firstly, I didn't find a mentor who had more experience and better words of encouragement. Secondly, I pursued the friendship with Negative Nancy 1 despite the fact that she wasn't speaking the language I knew would get me ahead. Don't make the mistakes I made. Find yourself a mentor and drop Negative Nancy, Debby Downer, Doubtful Thomas and Petisha McPetty. If your "Power Posse" doesn't give you power then perhaps you have a "Pull Down Posse". Fix it!

QuickFix Activity

- Assess the 5 closest persons in your life (friends and family); are they a "power posse" or "pulldown posse"?

- Keep the answer to yourself but if they are the latter – fix it.

SO WHAT NOW?

Have you been jerked into action as yet? After reading all the chapters of this book you should now know what you need to do to either get your business started or to move your existing business into the realm of success. Think about it! You are no less than all those successful business owners you know and admire. The only difference is that they employ different strategies from you, some of which I would have written about in this book.

Now you need to take action. Stop sitting on the sidelines while your fellow entrepreneurs are winning. Why be a spectator? Get in the game! Employ these strategies and I can guarantee you that in less than 12 months you will see a big difference in your output, your finances and general level of motivation. If you still feel stuck or crippled with fear visit my website www.nikkimeeks.com and sign up to receive your free consultation and let me help you to move to the next level.

The Secret to Entrepreneurial Success is the handbook that every small to medium sized business owner should carry. It's concise, unpretentious and to the point while touching a number of pain points for many entrepreneurs. From building a purpose-driven business to evaluating your business progress, Nikki takes entrepreneurs on a journey that is bound to revive their confidence and drive. Curl up with this short and spicy debut book but not without your notebook and pen because you are sure to gather enough information to propel you to next level business success.

About the Author

Nikki was born in the West Indies on the tiny island of Jamaica. She grew up in the capital city of Kingston. After high school, she pursued a teaching career and taught at the secondary level for approximately 4 years. She, however, had an intense passion for the field of business and switched career soon after to the insurance field.

Nikki progressed through the insurance arena from salesman to trainer to manager. As a salesman, she walked away with a number of awards putting her among the best in her company. When she left the insurance field she moved to the USA where she became an entrepreneur; owning and co-owning a number of small businesses.

Nikki is the proud mother of two lovely children; Jude and Chesni-Rae. With whom she enjoys traveling and exploring the great outdoors. She lives by the mantra "if you can do it, I can do it too", seeking motivation from those who have blazed a trail.